IT'S 3 AM & I CAN'T USE THE BUZZSAW

ANXIETY, MENTAL HEALTH & ME

Kevin Davies

First published in the United Kingdom in 2022 by Kevin Davies

Text copyright © Kevin Davies, 2022
Cover image copyright © Oladimeji, 2022
Editor: Ali Chambers

All rights reserved.

No part of this publication may be reproduced, distributed, or transmitted in any form or by any means, including photocopying, recording, or other electronic or mechanical methods, without prior written permission of the publisher, except in the case of brief quotations embodied in reviews and certain other non-commercial uses permitted by copyright law.

The moral rights of the author have been asserted.

DISCLAIMER: The information in this book is intended for educational and entertainment purposes only. This book is not intended to be a substitute for the medical or psychological advice of a professional. The author is not offering professional services advice. You should seek the services of a competent professional, especially if you need expert assistance for your specific situation. The author assumes no responsibility for your actions and specifically disclaim responsibility for any liability, loss, risk, or any physical, psychological, emotional, financial or commercial damages, personal or otherwise, which is incurred as a consequence, directly or indirectly, of the use and application of any of the contents of this book.

I would like to dedicate this book, first of all, to my Pickle, my wife, or many of the other names I have for her.
Others will know her as Phill.

Second, to my best friend, Dan, whose idea it was to turn my journaling into a book to help others.

Contents

Introduction	vii
1. You are in control	1
2. The ripple effect	17
3. "We grow through what we go through."	25
4. It's OK not to be OK	35
5. "What doesn't challenge you doesn't change you."	45
Acknowledgements	53
About the Author	55

Introduction

"It's in our darkest hours that we must focus to see the light." – Aristotle Onassis

It was about one-thirty on a Wednesday afternoon when my dad phoned me to tell me he was in the hospital. He'd had a suspected heart attack. He casually told me not to worry and that everything would be OK.

As it turned out my dad was right, everything was OK. Except for the bit where I had a mental breakdown. I didn't know how to cope. The thought of my dad not being around led to sleepless nights and not eating, which led to fatigue and the constant state of what I call 'triggered'. I was permanently on edge and got slapped with the harsh reality that; life goes on. I still had to work, bills still came in, and I still needed to function with the day-to-day challenges of life.

This isn't a book about my life story or my dad's. It's a short book about how I deal with my anxiety and my own mental health, in the hope that you'll find something that you can use to help with your own anxiety. It's a book to try and be the ripple effect for someone else, so that no one else feels as low or as out of control as I feel when my anxieties have taken over. This book has also been written to highlight the importance of recognising and staying in touch with your own mental health.

THERE IS NOTHING MORE IMPORTANT THAN YOUR MENTAL HEALTH

I want you to realise that anxiety is a feeling (or disorder) that you don't need to be afraid of. There's no reason to be, providing that you own it. Do not let it stop you from being the best version of yourself. Take the time to learn your triggers. But more importantly, learn about the resolution of those triggers. Because once you control your anxiety, you can calm it.

Anxiety has been a part of my entire adult life. I'm now nearly thirty-nine years old, and it's only recently that I've accepted it as a part of me. As I've taken the time to learn about myself, I feel stronger than ever and confident that I can tackle my challenges head-on.

That's not to say my ways of tackling anxiety are "right". These techniques I'm about to share with you are just what work for me. These are what I know and believe to work based on trial and error. I am not a therapist or a doctor. I am just a regular guy with a car, a mortgage and an 8–5 job that has taken the time to figure out what works for me. If you are struggling or do need help, reach out to a professional who can put you on a path that works for you. Don't do what I did for almost fifteen years and simply live with it.

Arthur Ashe said it best; "Start where you are. Use what you have. Do what you can."

1. You are in control

When I was twenty-one, I had my first panic attack. Now aged thirty-nine, I want to reassure you that if you put in the work, and have the right tools, you can control these. By control I mean recognise your feelings, adapt and overcome. Don't let them get the better of you. You deserve more.

My dad's heart attack was the final straw for me. That was the moment I knew that by not owning my anxiety, I was simply cheating myself out of the life I deserve.

I spent the best part of eight years worrying about when my next anxiety attack was coming. Every time my heart raced a bit faster than normal, every time I did something that wasn't routine, I'd start to hyperventilate. I'd catastrophise it into an event that wasn't happening before breathing rapidly and pacing around the house. Constantly playing out every possible scenario to my now wife, Phill.

Eventually, I'd wear myself out and, nine times out of ten, pass out where I was standing.

The first thing I tried to help me control my attacks was the brown bag technique.

For those of you that don't know, this is literally what it says on the tin. It's where you get a brown paper bag and breathe slowly into it. Slow deep breaths; in, out, in, out. Really focusing on the deep breaths.

Unfortunately for me, it just winds me up. The noise of the bag doesn't feel like it's in sync with what I'm trying to achieve. I don't have any noise filters, so when I go into a room I hear all of the conversations and noises. This gets me overwhelmed and the brown bag technique just adds more noise to an already noisy room. But that's me.

Try it for yourself. It has worked for so many others and is so simple. If you're not sure where to get a brown bag from, a fish shop/aquatics centre will stock them. They put the fish in them to keep them calm during transport.

When the brown paper bag didn't work, I quit drinking alcohol.

Between the ages of eighteen to twenty-one, I was like any other young adult. Mondays, Thursdays, and Saturday nights out. Jack Daniels, vodka, and even the legendary WKD Blue were my drinks of choice. I would have a night out, come home a tad worse for wear, and then wake up without a hangover.

By twenty-two, I was starting to have hangovers and let's just say I wasn't a fan.

So when I had my first attack I thought, maybe it was the drink. I had been drinking a lot and I felt so out of control that it scared me. As the brown bag hadn't worked, I decided to try and cut down the drinking that so many of us see as a normal part of life.

This wasn't a hard choice for me for two reasons. The first was that I didn't like hangovers, they were nasty. The second was that I had just completed my three-year apprenticeship with Porsche and I was now old enough to drive them. I wasn't prepared to lose my driving licence and risk my career because I'd had one too many the night before.

I still drink every now and then but I honestly couldn't tell you the last time I was drunk. I only had two rums and a Pimm's on my wedding day and the rest was water. But as the attacks happen when I'm sober, I know it's not the drink that triggers them. I choose to avoid getting drunk as I feel I have more control of myself when sober, therefore the attack can't escalate.

When the more severe attacks would happen, Phill would have to call ambulances out to our house. If your attacks are so bad that you need to call an ambulance, don't be afraid. Mental health is a real thing and an actual illness. We live in an extremely fast world with so much input that our brains can't cope.

When the ambulance first turned up, all I could do was apologise. Over and over again. I believed they had better things to do and people that were actually sick to look after. But the paramedics were outstanding. There was no judgement, just help when I needed it most. Let's face it, if you're having an attack, the worst thing someone can do is tell you to calm down.

Similar to the brown bag, the paramedics just put an oxygen mask on me and monitored my heart. They helped me focus on my breathing all the while confirming that my heart rate was normal and wasn't going to shoot out of my chest, even though that's what it felt like. They would supply me with oxygen, but I wasn't actually dealing with what was going on.

As I said earlier, often when I'd had an attack I would pass out. Then I would usually get a few hours of sleep before waking up as normal. I'd ignorantly think to myself, "At least I didn't die."

I would apologise to Phill and we would spend the next few days figuring out what triggered my attack. All the while, I'd feel so sick I'd stop eating. This would then leave me tired because I had no energy, which would start the whole cycle again.

Unfortunately for me, from the age of twenty-two, my attacks were more frequent. I think if I kept count, I was probably having one or two attacks a month.

They'd usually happen after the actual event that I was worried about when the world was quiet and my thoughts were louder. They were at three am when I couldn't use the buzzsaw to distract myself with my woodworking, so I had to take the time to find a resolution. Hence the title and writing of this book, but I'll cover that later.

Now, it's probably been about five years since I've had a full-blown attack.

I've had the feeling that an attack is happening in the years since, but I've gathered control before the attack can spiral. That's come from owning it. I don't hide the fact I have anxiety, I sometimes joke about it, but what I do is constantly look for opportunities every day to level up. I have a burning desire to improve myself physically, mentally, and emotionally every single day. This takes energy for me to do and I don't have time to be negative or have a victim mentality. I'm the only one that can change it.

There isn't a person walking this planet who hasn't had issues. After all, as humans, we are problem solvers. It's not for me to say someone has had it harder or easier than me. We should all be respectful of one another because we are all on our own journeys.

All I have to do is worry about myself. The rest is unnecessary worry and takes too much energy away. If I'm looking after myself, I can look after those I care about the most.

In hindsight, I now realise that I spent far too much energy focusing on the cause and have never needed to know the trigger of my anxiety. I wasted too much energy focusing on things out of my control. The attack had passed, so who cared? Why waste energy on an event that had already happened? I couldn't change the outcome. What I needed to know was actually; how do I prevent it from happening again?

WHAT CAN YOU DO TO GET A HANDLE ON THIS?

So, Phill and I didn't need an ambulance or to sit in A&E for four hours, taking doctors away from physical injuries, just to be told I was having a panic attack.

What I knew was that I didn't want to spend days after an attack being emotionally drained and apologising, not wanting to eat. I didn't want to stay in the vicious cycle of being anxious and fatigued with life just accepting it as the norm.

So that's the first step; acknowledging what you DON'T WANT.

The next is acknowledging what you DO WANT.

I wanted Phill and I to have a life we were grateful for. I have never wanted a normal life, to me normal is boring. I wanted a blessed life where I could grow old as a person knowing that I gave life my best shot. I wanted memories of places I've been, not places I've seen. I wanted to know that I had been a good person and that someone's day had been made better because I had taken the time to engage with them.

Every one of us has the potential to be incredible humans. All we have to do is get to know ourselves. Our strengths, our weaknesses and exactly what makes us tick.

Task: Acknowledging what you do want / Acknowledging what you don't want

Take the time to write out what you don't want to continue happening in your life:

You are in control 9

Now, if you could flip this on its head, what would your dream life look like:

What are your strengths?

You are in control 11

What are your weaknesses?

What do you need to work on in order to make your dream life a reality? Break it down into baby steps. Every step counts as a step forward to your dream life!

"YOU BETTER START LIKING YOURSELF."

You are the only person you are one hundred percent going to spend the rest of your life with.

On my journey with anxiety, I have tried all sorts of things to get a diagnosis and remove anxiety from my life. I've tried visits to the doctors to be told I've got seasonal asthma. I've had GPs prescribe beta-blockers. (I didn't want these as I figured it was a wiring in my head issue). I've tried not drinking alcohol. I've tried avoiding certain social situations, all while refusing to accept that anxiety is a part of me.

That was until I realised if I didn't accept that I have anxiety, I couldn't help others find what works for them. And without anxiety, I wouldn't have decided to pick up the phone to a twenty-four hour helpline that pointed me in the direction of CBT (Cognitive Behavioural Therapy) and to the best tool that works for me; grounding.

Grounding is a tool that I use when I feel anxious. It's a tool put in place to bring me into the present. It helps me stop worrying about things that haven't happened yet and to stop catastrophising.

I want to share with you what the beginning of my attacks feel like and what I do once my battle with an attack has kicked in.

I'm grounding, straight away. For me, grounding is a godsend. Once the shivers and sweats have started or the thoughts have started to spiral, once the tight feelings in my chest are coming into action, I have a choice to make. Fight or flight.

I can tell you now that fight is the better of the two options. Flight is just ignoring it. But with grounding, we can fight those tight feelings anxiety brings. We are always stronger with a solid foundation and grounding sets us up to prepare for a bit of a battle. After all, it's not good for us to be comfortable *all* of the time.

We have to stop our automatic thoughts from taking over. To bring ourselves back to the present where nothing is actually happening other than our thoughts. To do this, we use our senses. Our senses are simple and thankfully they are with us wherever we go. Sight, sound, smell, touch and taste.

For example, when I'm asleep and a trigger wakes me, the first thing I do is pause. I take a deep breath and I touch things that are in the bed. I touch the pillow and say out loud, "That's soft." I touch the headboard, "That's hard and cold". I'll get up and touch the radiator; "Hard and warm."

Then I tap my chest in a rhythmic state going with the beat of my heart and say "I'm OK." I continue with the chest-beating as it confirms that my heart is going at a normal rate, not the 100mph I think it is.

I then say out loud the things I see. The light switch, Phill, the crack in the paint where I need to decorate, anything. Just confirm it to yourself by saying it out loud.

Already, I'm calming myself, my thoughts are no longer spiralling. I'm controlling this. I can smell the lavender spray to help me sleep, I can hear the cat's snoring, the fish tank pump, and the fridge downstairs. Even something as simple as a dripping tap and I'm now back in the room.

If I'm struggling to ground, I will shower. I find it quite peaceful and calming to write positive affirmations on the shower glass if an attack has escalated. If it's gone too far, I find shower meditation is great. Warm water, steam and I write nice words on the glass in the shower. I can feel myself grounding as the water alters my breathing.

This doesn't have to work immediately; you can keep repeating it until the anxiety reduces. The directive here is to become present and to begin to learn to control your thoughts. I invite you to try grounding or shower affirmations the next time you feel your thoughts spiralling to see if it works for you.

What are some nice words you can write to yourself on the shower glass?

2. The ripple effect

As I write this, I'm sitting in Ilfracombe Harbour and I'm triggered. I'm feeling anxious because I've had a tiring, full-on couple of days with Phill and my best friend Dan. I'm overwhelmed and struggling to process what I've done to deserve two of the most incredible humans I've ever met. I'm blessed with these two people. They're my bookends who keep me upright when I'm about to fall. Both of them believe that I can help others by sharing my experience, which is why I'm writing this book.

Dan has taught me to learn about myself and they've both taught me to love the person I am. It's not to say I don't have faults; we all have those. But I'm trying, and both of them keep me striving to be better.

Now, Dan is very good at introducing me to things that I wouldn't usually do. He's the one that suggested I write this book instead of watching TV when I'm feeling like I'm going to have an attack. He's shown me things that I wouldn't think of myself, the things outside my comfort zone that aren't in my normal routine. Believe it or not, simple things like YouTube or Instagram. It's not in me to just browse, I'm a doer and I learn from doing. If you told me ten times to do something I wouldn't understand. Show me once and I'll remember it forever.

If you've got anyone fighting your corner, giving you that safe space to be you, then your journey is made easier. But that doesn't mean you can't do it alone. You just need the right tools and a nudge in the right direction. So this is where I get to be Dan for you and encourage you to do something outside of your comfort zone.

This brings me to my next anxiety tool; journaling.

I was introduced to videos on YouTube about understanding the power of the mind and the immense effects of journaling. Our minds are extremely powerful. The trouble is they get filled with things that aren't real. The beauty of journaling is that it allows us to get our thoughts out into the world and create room in our minds.

When you put pen to paper the word becomes real and it feels like a release. Have you ever heard something you don't like and then gone on a full-blown rant? That's essentially what journaling is but instead of

The ripple effect 19

saying it, you write it and because it's written you can evaluate it.

There is no hearsay of he said, she said. Just words that you wrote down which you can then elaborate on afterwards. You can write down frustrations, you can write down your blessings, you can write anything you like to clear some room in your mind.

Once I've been triggered and I've gone through grounding to bring myself into the present, I start writing. First, I acknowledge my automatic thoughts by writing them out. I know that for me to settle, I need to get them out of my head. Otherwise, I'll just add to them.

When I journal I tend to write my worries, then my automatic thoughts, and once I've calmed down, the actual outcome and how it made me feel. It's a much more productive way of airing my frustrations or counting my blessings. When I'm finished I can throw it away or action it if needed. I tend to keep the gratitude and throw the frustrations away as it comes back to the question; "Does it deserve my energy?" Journaling forces me to acknowledge that question and clears my mind.

The easiest way of doing this is a mind dump. This is where you grab your pen and paper or your laptop and you write down every single thought that is going through your mind. From worrying about your loved ones to the flag outside the window that's blowing in the breeze and stopping you from sleeping. Every single thought.

What we're trying to do is clear your mind. Trust me, you can feel that clarity as each thought is put to paper. You will feel your mind emptying and all of a sudden things will become clearer. You need that clarity to deal with what's going on.

A YouTuber called Struthless made a good analogy about it; think of your mind as a milk bottle. You have to empty it to see clearly.

I find that once I've written my automatic thoughts, I can read them back over. I can read them over and over until I realise that most of them are thoughts of events that have never happened or if they have, I can do bugger all to fix or change them. There is a quote from Winston Churchill about an old man on his deathbed: "He looks back at his worries and had a lot of troubles in his life, most of which had never happened." This is just like me and anxiety. I have a hundred possible outcomes triggering me before I've even started doing what I'm worried about. Tell me that's not a waste of energy! Worrying like this can easily take away opportunities given to me.

By putting pen to paper, I've created a process. I've evaluated my thoughts and looked at how they made me feel, which in turn has acknowledged my feelings. I've created clarity.

What I know now is that I'm extremely bad at understanding my feelings and this is where my anxiety comes from. It's FEAR; False Emotions Appearing Real. I misunderstand a feeling and it spirals.

That's why it's so important to do the grounding first, then to clear the mind. If our minds are not clear, nor is our vision of what is real and we can't move forward.

Once I've cleared my mind, I can move on to the next step in my process with anxiety. The last thing I want to do is top up my thoughts with more thoughts. I'm trying to stop being overwhelmed, right? So, after all that's been going on with the thoughts in my mind, I remind myself that I'm still here, I'm safe, and the flag that stopped me from sleeping and started all of this is still flapping in the wind. The waves are still flowing around the harbour and my heart is still beating.

Tomorrow will be a new day and a new opportunity to find what works for me. I am calm. The thoughts that triggered this episode don't matter. Let's look at those now.

Task: Mind dump your automatic thoughts

1. What's the situation that has triggered you? Explain it in as much detail as you wish.

2. Write out all of the automatic thoughts associated with the situation.

3. How are those thoughts making you feel?

4. Are these thoughts true? Is there a more balanced view, a 'truer thought', you could believe right now? What is that?

5. How do you feel reading back the 'truer thought'?

The ripple effect 23

Here's a whole free page to journal on your thoughts. Use the prompts from the previous page to help you get started.

3. "We grow through what we go through."
Dhiman

As you're taking the time to read this far, and trying out these techniques, I'm sure you're finding what works for you be it medicinal or not. The beauty is that there isn't a right or wrong, it's simply about what will work for you. That's what's great with us all being different and the sooner you stop worrying about what others think, the better. The right people will support you; the wrong people will show themselves for what they are and you can move on.

When I first went to the doctor, he wanted to prescribe me things to take the edge off. I simply took the tablets with me and used them once before a night out. I don't even remember what they were called as I decided right then and there that they weren't fixing the issue. All I was doing with tablets was masking over the cracks.

I used to be complacent with my attacks. I'd think, 'I've had my attack, let's just crack on as normal.' But if you're reading this, you know that a panic attack isn't a one-time thing. I needed to untangle my mind and figure out some healthy habits that I could put into practice in my day-to-day life. This was probably my biggest hurdle, I needed to consistently work on one thing; me.

Then, my dad's heart attack turned my world upside down.

He's my best friend and has been there for me my entire life. He taught me right from wrong, to be a good human, and to never quit. His tips for life were to; have a smart haircut, clean shoes and a firm handshake. With these three things and manners, you could achieve anything he told me.

Since his heart attack, my dad has added "It is what it is" to any problem and I think this makes him almost untouchable. He's content and blessed with each new day. It allows him to focus on the important things. I'm trying to take more of that approach with me on my journey.

The thought of my dad not being around simply terrified me and I didn't know how to cope. I had other things going on in life as well. I was working 8–5, sometimes 8–8 to keep myself busy and get work done. There were many changes happening at work; if you haven't guessed by now, I'm a worrier by nature. That's when I reached out for CBT, when the reality of life all got too much.

As previously mentioned, I'm not a doctor nor do I have the qualifications to say this will work for you. But CBT is an approved therapy that has allowed me to invest in myself fully and grow as an individual living with mental health issues.

After many years of anxiety attacks (even though I was open about having them) I was still very reserved about how frequent they were and to what extent.

After my dad's heart attack, if I wasn't working, I was going to St Georges to visit Dad. I was reading about the possible outcomes and, as I was prone to do, I was thinking the worst. We were also awaiting results on a cancer scare for my stepmum who had been cancer-free for a long time. Jackie (my stepmum) and Phill were my rocks when Dad was in the hospital, but no matter what they said, I wasn't listening.

So at two am on a Wednesday morning I phoned a Bupa helpline. I got a call back from a psychiatrist after explaining what was happening. She replied, "You've got a lot going on, haven't you love?" I broke down in tears. Someone had finally heard me. I didn't even get her name but she opened the door to CBT, so thank you.

I realise I'm extremely blessed because I get Bupa (health insurance) for free with my work. It took one appointment with my GP to refer me privately for

CBT, and I had my first session a week later. Unfortunately, it's not that quick with the NHS in England but it *is* available and done to the same level. Here in England, a lot of doctors, nurses, and psychiatrists that work in the private healthcare sector also work for the NHS. The main difference is where you are treated and the speed you can get seen.

Having CBT for me was life-changing because my psychiatrist, Andrew, was completely impartial. He took the time to find out more about me and gave me the huge reality check I needed. He showed me that I wasn't just not coping with my dad, but I wasn't coping with life. I was burning myself out by saying yes to too many people whilst sacrificing my own health. If I didn't change my ways my life would continue like this.

CBT gives you the tools to cope with your mental health issues. It is non-medicinal and really allows you to grow as a person. The hardest thing about it is picking up the phone. After that, you have impartial support.

Even if you don't have supportive people around you, you can get professionals. The call handler at Bupa and Andrew were the two who really helped me start my journey of change. And if I can be that little difference to one person with this book, in this up and down adventure we call life, I'll die a happy man.

CBT taught me that it's OK to not be OK. We all need a little support sometimes. After all, you can't pour from an empty cup. If you're not looking after yourself, how on earth are you going to help your loved ones?

For CBT to work, we have to make some life changes. To realise that self-care isn't a bad thing. It isn't selfish. Here are fifteen other cognitive errors I learned from CBT that most of us let our brains do when we aren't actively keeping them in check.

Filtering: taking negative details and magnifying them, while filtering out all positive aspects of a situation.

Polarised thinking: thinking of things as black or white, good or bad, perfect or failure, with no middle ground.

Overgeneralisation: jumping to a general conclusion based on a single incident or piece of evidence; expecting something bad to happen over and over again if one bad thing occurs.

Mind reading: thinking that you know, without any external proof, what people are feeling and why they act the way they do; believing yourself able to discern how people are feeling about you.

Catastrophising: expecting disaster; hearing about a problem and then automatically considering the possible negative consequences (e.g., "What if tragedy strikes?" "What if it happens to me?").

Personalisation: thinking that everything people do or say is some kind of reaction to you; comparing yourself to others, trying to determine who's smarter or better looking.

Control fallacies: feeling externally controlled as helpless or a victim of fate or feeling internally controlled, responsible for the pain and happiness of everyone around.

Fallacy of fairness: feeling resentful because you think you know what is fair, even though other people do not agree.

Blaming: holding other people responsible for your pain or blaming yourself for every problem.

Shoulds: having a list of ironclad rules about how you and other people "should" act; becoming angry at people who break the rules and feeling guilty if you violate the rules.

Emotional reasoning: believing that what you feel must be true, automatically (e.g., if you feel stupid and boring, then you must be stupid and boring).

Fallacy of change: expecting that other people will change to suit you if you pressure them enough; having to change people because your hopes for happiness seem to depend on them.

Global labelling: generalising one or two qualities into a negative global judgement.

Being right: proving that your opinions and actions are correct on a continual basis; thinking that being wrong is unthinkable; going to any lengths to prove that you are correct.

Heaven's reward fallacy: expecting all sacrifice and self-denial to pay off as if there were someone keeping score, and feeling disappointed and even bitter when the reward does not come.

In CBT, I realised how often I was letting my mind control me rather than the other way around. How was I going to help my dad if I couldn't help myself?

I'm now in a place where I know he won't be around forever, but none of us will. So now I make the time to be happy and enjoy life with my loved ones. Whilst I know that life can be overwhelming, I also know that being on edge all the time and overthinking every situation isn't sustainable. Life is a marathon, not a sprint. We have to pace ourselves and get to know how we function.

This is where my daily distractions come in. When I'm not feeling anxious, I need to feel content and calm. I need to figure out how to balance life and stop the anxiety from kicking in. I have to try for a constant form of "I'm OK" every day.

My distractions have many forms. They are both mental and physical. Sometimes they involve doing things, sometimes they involve nothing but resting. Either way, I have to be present, I have to acknowledge my surroundings and how I'm feeling as I did in the previous chapters.

You have to be aware of what you're thinking and what you're doing to find the right distraction for you. It's all too easy to autopilot through each day, but that's when life catches up with you and anxiety can sneak up on you. To find the right distractions you have to strip your thoughts back and find what feels good.

This isn't a task to find what you're good at, this is a task to find what you *enjoy*. None of us are born good at anything. We find an interest and we practise it to become good. Once we're good at it, we practise more to maintain our levels or better ourselves even more.

Task: Discovering your distractions

List out some things that could improve your mood every day and take your mind away from all the events and situations in your head that you're worried about, but have never actually happened.

4. It's OK not to be OK

Now, a week after I've returned from Ilfracombe, I'm still processing and dealing with my last anxiety attack. I use attacks as an alarm clock that I need a time-out in general. I know I'm worse when I'm tired.

I was triggered in Devon and I went through my grounding and journaling. As it never escalated, and a week passed, I had the time to reflect. More importantly, I had the time to process it and process it properly because it was all written down.

When Phill went to work I jumped on the Ducati and headed to my happy place; the ocean. When I'm on my bike all of the tabs in my mind close and I'm free. On this occasion, I rode to East Wittering beach armed with a coffee flask, gold bar, and a cheese & pickle sandwich. Then I simply sat there for a while listening to the waves crashing on the shore. The sun was beating down on my face and I was at peace because I was in nature doing something I wanted to do.

My bike is a great distraction and I'm not going to lie, it's the most fun, but I need more than one. You will too. After all, what happens when the anxiety attack starts at three am? When I can't use the buzzsaw and distract myself with woodworking another one of my distractions. What am I supposed to do then?

It's simple, I'll put on the TV and watch a comedy. I'll put on music, I'll read a book, I'll go for a drive. I'll even load up my cat 'Asterix' and take him for a walk in my backpack.

Some people think it's weird I walk my cat but this is the great thing about me, I don't care because he's happy. I don't take him out up hills or on hikes over heathland to please others. I take him out because it's good for him. It's safer than leaving him wandering a housing estate and we both come back fulfilled. This is why I told you it was important you don't care what others think of you. It's about what makes YOU happy.

If the hours are more reasonable and I'm not going to affect others I will do my woodworking. I'll clean the car and bikes, go for a bike ride, go to the gym, or go fishing with my dad. All of the above things I enjoy doing. They give me a lift and take me away from the overthinking that usually spirals into anxiety. The list is long because they are all things I enjoy.

Go back over your list from the last chapter now and make sure you have something for any time, day or night, that you could do. It could even be something as simple as crosswords if that's what you like.

As I said, woodworking is my go-to. I enjoyed it at school, I'm OK at it, but most of all it keeps me grounded. It increases my 'feel goods' as well as my skills. And, as you can tell, it's the reason behind the title of this book.

I love to pick up a piece of wood and just create something. I've built birdhouses, bug hotels, TV units, candle holders, all sorts. It just gives me pure joy that once I've finished, I gift it to someone else. I always say, if you don't like it, it'll make great firewood. Because it's not the end piece I enjoy, it's the process. That piece of wood has done its job, it's created calm in my mind.

All I'm doing is putting my mental health first and giving myself an alternative thing to think about other than the hyperventilating thoughts that usually go through my mind.

It's really all about simplifying your life and creating healthy habits. It's too easy to go on social media, like a meme or a quote, and think that you're coping. The harsh reality is we're not. We're merely existing autonomously.

Ever heard of the saying reel life vs real life? It's a reflection of what's portrayed on social media vs how we are day to day. People rarely post something negative and as humans, we end up comparing. We feel worthless and like we're achieving less than that person on Instagram. In reality, they could be having a bad day too but the photo looks like they're living their best life.

To get a handle on things we have to put in the work, we have to realise that self-care isn't selfish and we have to find ways to increase our mood. That's the hardest thing because so many of us expect to just become good at something without putting in the work.

The way that I look at it is that the mind is a muscle. For me to improve my mental state, I have to work at it. Just like an athlete trains their body to be the best, I need to train my mind.

This happens when we become present with what makes us feel good. When we take away the commute, the bad day at work, or the negatives constantly streamed on the media. Only when we've taken away the negative distractions can we really find what brings us real happiness.

Take all of those away and find some time for yourself. This is when you can really start to understand what's going on in your mind and this is why it's so important to find the right distraction for you.

If you're not sure where to start, figure out what makes you smile. What actually brings you moments of joy.

Usually, we know when we are down or anxious but it's very hard to figure out why. I've had moments where

I've felt completely empty and numb and for the life of me have no explanation why; my life's good and I'm truly blessed.

What sometimes happens is we simply burn out. For me, it could just be something small that has spiralled because I've failed to acknowledge it. Don't get me wrong, this doesn't take away from those big things happening. But there's no point wasting energy on things you can't impact.

My dad's heart attack taught me that life is precious and I want to live it. I don't want to just exist. I'm a lucky one, my dad survived. He's different and he has his own struggles, but we are closer than ever. For this, I'm eternally grateful.

I've discovered finding positive things in a day lifts my mood. I actively start with the smallest of things. It can be having running hot water, a nice cup of tea, a gentle breeze or just a smile from a stranger.

WHAT IS IT ABOUT THESE ACTIVITIES THAT ACTUALLY MAKE US FEEL GOOD?

Dopamine. This is the chemical reward for our bodies. The way we increase our dopamine levels is by celebrating the little wins. Eat good food, take part in self-care activities like hot showers, meditation or mindfulness etc. We even get it by completing a task. That could be a crossword or a project you decided to start. You choose.

For me, this is my woodwork where I'll build what I like to call rustic pallet builds. The fact I can build homes for nature gives me a huge sense of achievement. It doesn't cost me anything but time and tools, and it makes me feel good once it's finished.

If this is well above your skill set, you could even sort out the cupboards that you've constantly been putting off. Either way, your dopamine levels will increase.

Next up is Oxytocin. This generally comes from others or pets, but even simply hugging your family or playing with pets can give you a lift. Holding hands and giving compliments can also help lift your mood. Oxytocin is, after all, the love hormone.

This is why I'm grateful for Asterix, my cat. If I don't feel like doing anything, the boy gives me the best cuddles.

The third is my favourite chemical; Serotonin. This is the mood stabiliser. I increase these levels by running, which isn't my favourite exercise but does allow me time in the sun. I can also increase it by walking with nature, swimming, meditating, cycling, all sorts. I love finding ways to increase my levels. Just look at the word nature. It's natural and I'm sure that's where I'm most at peace.

Pass the time by being outside and you'll be lifted with a pure sense of things to be grateful for.

Last of all is endorphins. These are the body's painkillers. Probably the hardest thing on the list, but probably the quickest mood lifter. It's not to say it's easy but exercise has so many benefits both physically and mentally, and it releases the most endorphins.

I do regular gym work to stay strong but more importantly to improve my mental health. After a workout, my mind is fully charged, which far outweighs the physical gains. The hardest thing is going in.

That's not to say that a piece of dark chocolate or watching a funny programme won't also give you a lift.

Look for the good things in your life that bring these feelings of accomplishment, love, mood-boosting and endorphins, and more good things will appear. They happen every day but we lose sight of them with all of the negativity that surrounds us.

In general, I find it will take me five positives to remove one negative. That's why I rarely watch the news or buy a newspaper. The media focuses too much on the awful things going on in the world and it gives me a huge sense of injustice. That's not to say good things aren't happening, but I've never heard a reporter share what's being done to solve the problem.

Have you? No. They just fuel us with more negatives. So, if it's out of your circle of influence then acknowledge your emotions and move on.

Task: Five positive thoughts for every one negative thought

You may find it takes more than five positives, but start looking for the good things in a day. Use the template below and give it a go:

One negative thought. How did it make me feel?

1.

Five positive thoughts. How did they make me feel?

1.

2.

3.

4.

5.

By creating my own positive mindset, it helps my mood stay more stable and reduces my catastrophising. I still acknowledge that bad things happen. But working daily on the positives means I know where to look when my moods get lowered. In general, if my mood is lifted, I find my anxiety is massively reduced and therefore my mental health is increased.

As you can see there are many ways to increase your mood and in turn reduce your anxiety but they all have a vital ingredient; you. You have to put the work in. You have to own your anxiety and your mental health. By doing that, a beautiful life full of experience can be lived.

I guess what I'm trying to say out of all of this, is that you need to accept yourself. *For* yourself. There are so many things in this life that we don't like about ourselves but actually, by looking at ourselves in a different light we can really grow as people.

I used to think that I needed to hide my anxiety or the fact I had a breakdown. But I've now learnt that by being open and taking the time to understand it, I can actually make a difference to others.

Let's face it, everyone has gone through something. We've all been through a lot. But by trying to strengthen your mindset, you're trying to help yourself when something else comes up and challenges you.

There is no dress rehearsal for life. We can only play the cards we're dealt. Hopefully, by reading this you might find a better way of coping. After all, it's OK to not be OK.

5. "What doesn't challenge you doesn't change you."
Fred DeVito

Over the years I've tried a lot of things to 'fix' my anxiety. However, it's only come to light recently that if I make the hard decisions, that's when I feel most accomplished. I'm convinced there is a link between self-worth and anxiety. In my view, having little to no self-worth can be a huge part of the cause. That means, as a person I need to be better today than I was yesterday but worse than I'll be tomorrow.

I can be told time and time again that I'm "good at this" or "great at that" and I let it go over my head. That's been fuel to the fire, and it's only now that I actually reaffirm positives that are said to me and that helps to increase my confidence.

Throughout my life, I've people pleased to fit in. It was only recently that I decided to remove people from my life that weren't bringing anything to the table. That's been one of the toughest calls I've made but it's also proved to be the most valuable.

It's not that they are bad people or they are worth less than me, it's that I need my energy to improve myself. I can't afford to have someone else draining me or having a negative impact on my life. I pray that they get the help they need, but not to the detriment of my own health.

It's extremely hard to remove people from your life, especially when you're struggling. You may have that fear that you're going to be alone. If you're compassionate, you may worry about their feelings. But do you have that someone that rarely contacts you unless it's a reply to something you've sent? Do you have that person that only gets in touch when they need something? That person you dread talking to?

Think about the conversations you're having with people. Do they just gossip about others or constantly talk about the past? These are the people that are not only holding themselves back, but they're also holding you back.

What I'm saying is; surround yourself with the right people. Action the changes in your life to improve your confidence. When you realise that your vibe is your tribe, the people that are good for your life will find a way to be a part of it and you'll all start to bounce off each other.

"What doesn't challenge you doesn't change you." 47

I started to figure out who I wanted to share my journey of life with when I stopped messaging the ones I didn't. When I stopped checking in on others, I quickly figured out who was checking in on me. Of course, you have to appreciate that everyone is busy. But when it's one way, I've drawn the line.

Those true friends will notice the change in behaviour and contact you to make sure you're OK. You can tell them you're having a bit of a digital detox or you're trying to improve yourself and your mental health, and they will understand. If they don't then they aren't who you thought they were to you.

If you have that friend that's been a part of your life for so long they feel like family but they just drag you down, tell them. Tell them that their negative behaviour is affecting you and that you want to start sharing some positive experiences with them. Invite them on your walks, book a meal out, or even go to some exercise classes together and you'll both feel better. After all, they deserve a good life too.

Don't get into arguments. Respect other views. But as soon as someone starts insulting you or making you feel like crap, ghost them. There is nothing wrong with this and they need to look at the way they are behaving. If they're willing to address it, you can talk it out with them. But it's not your responsibility to judge others, so let them look at themselves.

Arguments accomplish nothing. Practise the pause and tell them how they've made you feel. They're your feelings to manage. Give it time and if it's a real friendship it'll fix itself and you'll both be stronger.

I've ghosted people. The result is I haven't spoken to them in years. But I know they are getting on with their life just as much as I'm getting on with mine.

I can tell you, there will be good days and bad days. But once you have your inner circle, you'll live your life in a bubble that makes you feel like you're unstoppable! This will prompt you to try more things because you don't feel like you're being judged. Your people simply don't care as long as you're trying your best. Once you start trying more, you'll see you start achieving more, and you start stepping out of your comfort zones. You'll find that you're more fulfilled as a person and you can encourage others with your own achievements.

As we live in a social media world full of likes, I have a little task for you. As I mentioned I'm not very good with social media, but I remember this post I read. I call it 100-10-5-2-1 because I've got about a hundred FB friends. I like my circles small.

When I'm in trouble or struggling, I put a post up. Out of my one hundred friends, I get ten comments or care hugs. Out of those ten comments, I get five text messages to check I'm OK. Once I've replied to those five messages, I get two phone calls to just be sure I'm alright and out of those two calls, I get one knock on the door.

If you have that one person that will knock on the door, you're winning, that's your person.

This is a rhetorical exercise and I'm not saying put a post out saying you need help. But figure out who will be there when you need it most; be it colleagues, acquaintances, mates, friends or partners. They are the ones that deserve your energy. There's nothing wrong if there is no one on that list right now.

I only met Dan about eight years ago on a motorbike forum when he said he was new to the area and asked if anyone fancied a ride out. I now see him as a little brother and he was the best man at my wedding. It's never too late to meet new people.

THE CHOICES YOU MAKE

As well as the people we choose to surround ourselves with, we also have day-to-day choices we have to make. It can be all too easy to pick the comfortable route, but that's not how we grow.

This is why now when I get up in the morning, the first thing I do is take a moment to check in with myself. How am I feeling, any aches, did I sleep well, what are today's goals? The list goes on. It's easier to check social media, but what does that achieve?

Here's one of my lists for a working day:

- How did I sleep? 7/10 Feel slightly refreshed.
- What will I do today that's just for me? 30 min walk along the river to work.
- What will I do today for someone else? Make tea for the parts department.
- What will I do to improve my physical health? 40 mins gym on the way home.
- What will I do today to improve my mental health? 15 mins meditation before bed. No blue light e.g. phones, laptops, iPad etc.
- What has been negative today? Traffic, plus workload was high.
- What has been positive today? The roof over my head, job to go to, vanilla oat milk latte, parts said thank you for tea, watching Asterix play, I took the time to walk the river and exercise.

I write this in the morning and then make sure I've got either my journal, my gym clothing or walking shoes with me. Whatever happens today, I need to find time to exercise or write. I could just wing it and see how the day plans out, but I'm in less control that way. By taking the above with me, I'm committing to making time to do something to better my health. Even on weekends, I get dressed in gym wear so I can go and exercise as I know it will give my mood a lift.

Once I'm at work, I write down a to-do list and prioritise each task with the numbers to reflect their level of importance. Once I've accomplished the task, I simply tick it off and add something else. This gives me that accomplishment.

TRY THE LIST FOR YOURSELF:

- How did you sleep?
- What will you do today that's just for you?
- What will you do today for someone else?
- What will you do to improve your physical health?
- What will you do today to improve your mental health?
- What has been negative today?
- What has been positive today?

Can you see how these small changes in your day-to-day life can give you that extra bit of control? It's said that it takes sixty-six days to build a habit, try it; what's the worst that could happen? These small adjustments stop you from just auto-piloting through the day, coming home to watch TV for three hours before going to bed and repeating it tomorrow.

You have twenty-four hours in a day, you have one thousand four hundred and forty minutes, or you have eighty-six thousand four hundred seconds if you like. That's enough time to challenge yourself to do something *for yourself*.

I was convinced I needed two hours to accomplish a gym session including travel. That's nonsense. I cut my workout to forty minutes from over an hour and by having gym gear with me I can go whilst I'm out. I was convinced I needed to sit for an hour for my lunch break in the tea room. Actually, I can walk for fifteen, sit for fifteen and then return with time to spare. It takes me out of the workplace and is technically me putting up my own 'do not disturb'. I'm having my time.

Hopefully, you can see that by making changes in your life you are prioritising yourself. When you start doing that, your eyes will be open to seeing that if you've been gifted today, don't waste it with worry. Or as my dad says, to realise "It is what it is."

Acknowledgements

Thank you for taking the time to read this. I want to give special thanks to my two bookends for their support, their listening ears, and constant encouragement to just be me. Without you two, who knows what would be going on?

Phill, we've been together since 2004 and the love, care and support I receive from you is what makes me the man I am today. You have been alongside me every step of the way and inspiring me to be a better version of myself each day.

Dan, without your belief that I could help others, and your faith in what I can do, I wouldn't have even attempted to write a book. You encourage me to step out of my comfort zone, believe in myself, and go after my dreams whilst remaining forever humble.

Acknowledgements

To my dad John and my stepmum Jackie, I can't envisage where my life would be without you. I have so much to be grateful for that I owe to you, but you never take any credit. You are always there for Phill and I and never expect anything in return. Thank you.

I also want to thank everyone involved in keeping my dad here today. You are unsung heroes who I will be eternally grateful for.

To Andrew White for giving me the tools with my CBT to realise that self-care isn't selfish. And to Ali for making this book real, a special talent. Without her, it would have stayed on my laptop.

To my tribe. My friends, my family. The ones that have been with me on this crazy journey we call adulthood. Good times and bad times, we're giving life a damn good go. You all mean the world to me and I'm truly blessed to have you all as a part of my life.

Finally, to every one of you who has read this and taken something from it that can help you cope. Wanting to grow as a person is the most important thing in this life and the more people that are learning how to improve themselves and take tools they can share with others, the better. I can't stress enough that if you're struggling, you need to talk to a professional. Don't feel like you're alone, there are great people out there to guide you.

Much love,

Kev

About the Author

Kevin Davies was born in '83 and brought up in Woking, Surrey with his mum, dad and sister. At eleven, after his parents' separation, Kevin went a bit off track. He didn't like school, didn't fit in, and generally found it easier to be the class clown rather than study. The only classes he liked were woodwork and P.E.

At fifteen, he had a run-in with the police and it was his dad and Jackie who made him realise without an education he wasn't going anywhere. He got his GCSEs, including a D in English literature. Here he is today with a published book.

His dad encouraged Kevin to get a trade skill, and once Kevin got over the fact he didn't want to get his hands dirty, he also learnt mechanics. In the twenty years since (after applying for apprenticeships with Honda, Porsche and false reliant robin, something that still makes Kev laugh), Kevin has fixed Porsches. During that time he won an apprentice of the year award, repaired, built and maintained some incredible cars, including a Boxster race car, and had some incredible driving experiences.

In his spare time, he loves getting out on his motorbikes, discovering new places and just generally getting lost. Well, not lost just an alternate route he probably couldn't find again. He also loves spending time with the recent addition to the family; Asterix. This boy knows when Kev is up or down, reminds him of himself, is pure mischief, and is always up to something.

Kevin's wish with this book is that it brings you one thing above all else: hope. If you can find hope in your life by realising that you're not alone and that you can achieve whatever you put your mind to, then this book has worked. After all, Kevin has written a book with a D in English Lit and has a career fixing cars with no experience of fixing cars. If he can do that, you can do or be anything you put your mind to.

Using the tools he has shared with you in this small book, hopefully, has encouraged you to push yourself out of your comfort zone and want more for yourself. You can see that your current situation isn't your final destination as long as you're willing to put in the work.

He is generally quite reserved on social media, but you will find Kevin, Phill & Asterix at @675peanuts on Instagram or @KevinDavies on Facebook. He is also in a private group on Facebook called The Anxiety Diaries, which you are welcome to join. It's a group set up by his friend Chrissy, for other people to have a safe space to talk and share their experiences.

Finally, if you've taken anything from this book, please leave a review as Kevin would love to hear of your successes in your own mental health.

Lightning Source UK Ltd.
Milton Keynes UK
UKHW020635231122
412703UK00017B/793